Debi Gliori's
Bedtime Stories

In memory of Leslie Gardiner –
writer, champion, and dear friend.

DK

A PENGUIN COMPANY
LONDON, NEW YORK, MUNICH,
MELBOURNE, and DELHI

First published in Great Britain in 2002
by Dorling Kindersley Limited,
80 Strand, London WC2R ORL

2 4 6 8 10 9 7 5 3 1
Text copyright © 2002 Debi Gliori
Illustrations copyright © 2002 Debi Gliori
The author's and illustrator's moral rights have been asserted.

A CIP catalogue record for this book is available from the British Library.

ISBN 0-7513-4577-6

Colour reproduction by Dot Gradations, UK
Printed and bound in China by Toppan Printing Co., Ltd.

see our complete
catalogue at
www.dk.com

Debi Gliori's
Bedtime Stories

Bedtime tales with a twist

DK

A Dorling Kindersley Book

Introduction

Assembling these nine stories into a collection was, if you'll forgive the domestic metaphor, a bit like making a nine-course dinner. All the ingredients were familiar: a little red hen, a ravenous wolf, a zippy hare, a sluggish tortoise, and… well, you probably have lots of them in your fridge or cupboards too.

How to use everyday ingredients and out of them make a dinner to remember? The trick, in books as in cooking, is twofold: the quality of the ingredients and what you do with them. Therefore, I picked my Little Red Hen carefully from the organic section, I chose only the most ravenously debonair of Wolves, I sourced my sluggish nose-in-a-book Tortoise with considerable effort, and I was all zipped out tracking down the perfect Hare. Like any cook with a dinner to make, I laid out my ingredients and tried not to panic. Nine courses – what could I have been thinking of?

730 days later, I've emerged pink and triumphant from the kitchen to bring you a small feast of stories laced with the literary equivalent of basil, garlic, fresh coriander, and a handful of fresh green chillies…
and, lest I forget, a very large pinch of salt.

Debi Gliori

Contents

Little Red Hen

In a little farm cottage at
The Back of Beyond lived a pig,
a cat, a duck, and The Little Red Hen.
Pig spent his days doing the crossword in
the paper, Cat spent her days sleeping and
sunbathing, and Duck lounged by the pond
making herself beautiful. And Little Red Hen?
Well, someone had to do all the work.
   Little Red Hen scrubbed, polished, vacuumed,
mowed, dug, weeded, shopped, cooked, and

did all the laundry from dawn to dusk, day in, day out, three hundred and sixty-five days a year.

"Where's my newspaper?" said Pig.

"Coming," said Little Red Hen.

"My bed needs making," yawned Cat.

"I'm on my way," said Little Red Hen.

"I'm starving," moaned Duck.

"I'll put lunch on in a minute," said Little Red Hen.

Poor Little Red Hen.

One night Little Red Hen went outside to milk the cows, lay some eggs, and close the greenhouse down for the evening. As she sat milking, she remembered a task that she'd left undone.

"HEAVENS!" she squawked. "I've forgotten to plant the corn. I wonder if my friends would help?"

Back she went into the house.

"I'm a wee bit tired," she said. "Would one of you help me to plant the corn?"

Pig waved his paper. "Not me. I'm stuck on 5 down. Four letters, rhymes with hazy, begins with an 'L'?"

Cat stretched by the fire. "Not me. What a lovely, *lazy* time I'm having…"

Duck looked round from the mirror. "Not me. I've got feathers to preen."

Little Red Hen sighed and went back outside. She milked the cow, laid some eggs, shut down the greenhouse, and then she sowed the corn. By the time she'd finished, it was nearly morning.

Time passed and the corn ripened. One night
Little Red Hen was ironing with the radio on.
She heard the weather forecaster say
that there was a storm approaching.

"GOOD GRIEF!" she squawked.
"I must harvest the corn before the
storm blows it flat. I wonder if
my friends would help?"

She opened the sitting room door and poked her head round.
"I'm exhausted," she sighed. "Would one of you help me to harvest
the corn?"

Pig gave a snort. "Not me. I've just begun another crossword. Listen
to this: 2 down, sounds like what a fishmonger does, seven letters?"

Cat hissed at Little Red Hen, "Not me. Don't be so *selfish* –
I was nearly asleep."

Duck muttered, "Not me. I have to pluck my duckbrows."

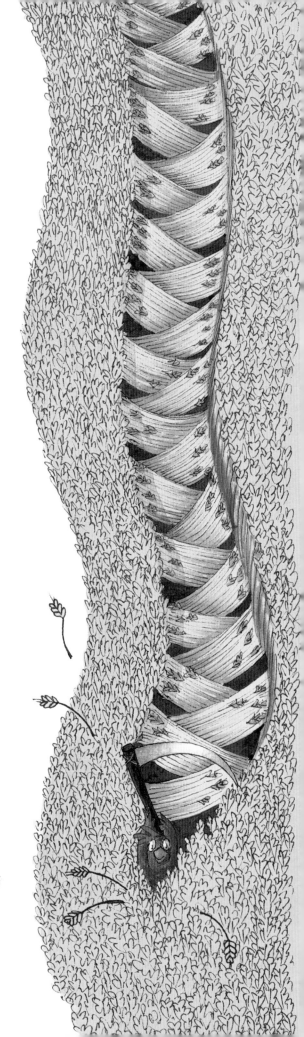

Little Red Hen groaned and headed for the front door. Wearily she picked up a scythe and staggered off to the cornfield. She harvested the corn, put it in sacks in the barn, and finished the ironing. By that time, the sun was streaming in through the kitchen windows, so Little Red Hen didn't bother to go to bed at all.

At six o'clock, she laid four perfect eggs and milked the cows.

At seven o'clock, she watered the plants in the greenhouse and picked four lemons.

At eight o'clock, she cooked breakfast, served it to her friends, and washed up afterwards.

"Toast was a bit too crispy," complained Pig. "Anyone know what 3 down might be? Sounds like sticky, begins with a small green vegetable?"

"Call me *picky*," whinged Cat, "but the porridge wasn't exactly up to scrrrratch, was it?"

"I'm still hungry," moaned Duck. "Isn't there any more?"

At nine o'clock, Little Red Hen vacuumed the house, made the beds, and cleaned the bathroom.

At ten o'clock, she polished the silver, dusted the ornaments, and defrosted the fridge.

At eleven o'clock, she collapsed in a chair.

"I'm shattered," she whimpered. "Surely my friends will help me out?"

Blinking in the bright sunshine, Little Red Hen dragged herself out to the pond where Pig, Cat, and Duck were draped across deck-chairs.

"I've been up all night," yawned
Little Red Hen. "I'm absolutely pooped. Please,
would one of you help me make some pastry?"

"Not me," sniggered Cat. "What a liar you are, Hen.
I saw you sit down in a chair two minutes ago…"

"Not me," sniffed Duck. "I hate getting my feathers all
covered in goop."

Little Red Hen looked at her friends. Something deep
inside her snapped.

"Rrrrright!" she said. "I'll do it myself. All of it."
And she stalked back into the house.

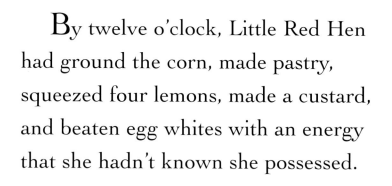

By twelve o'clock, Little Red Hen had ground the corn, made pastry, squeezed four lemons, made a custard, and beaten egg whites with an energy that she hadn't known she possessed.

At twelve thirty, she slid a perfect lemon meringue pie out of the oven and onto a plate.

At twelve forty-one and twenty seconds, she appeared at the pond.

"So," she said, dusting her floury feathers on her apron and licking a smear of something off her beak, "who will help me eat my lemon meringue pie?"

14

Pig leapt to his feet. His newspaper slid into the pond.

"ME!" he shouted. "I'd be delighted to help!"

Cat sprang to her paws. "ME!" she miaowed. "I'll help you right now!"

Duck fell off her deck-chair in her haste to be first at the house.

"ME!" she squawked. "Although I'd better not eat too much – it's so bad for the complexion."

"Well, lawks a mussy," drawled Little Red Hen. "What a helpful bunch my friends all are! But – what a shame. You wouldn't help me plant the corn. You wouldn't help me harvest it. You wouldn't help me make the pastry. I thought you wouldn't help me eat the lemon meringue pie. So I ate it all by myself. Without your help. And *mmm mmm*, it was *deeelicious!*"

Nail Soup

Hen stood in her brand-new kitchen in her brand-new house and sighed. In front of her were six hundred and forty-two cardboard boxes full of her worldly goods. So far, she'd only unpacked one box and found her soup pot, her chopping board and knife, and — would you believe it — one rusty nail. The doorbell rang and a voice called,

"Coo-eee! Anybody home?"

My new neighbour, thought Hen, running to open the door.

On the doorstep stood a large and scrawny fox.

"Good morning," he said. "Welcome to the neighbourhood, my dear. I just thought I'd pop round to ask you over for dinner tonight."

Hen was about to reply when Fox grabbed her, slammed the door shut behind himself and growled, "Nothing too elaborrrrate — just you and me. You'll be the one simmerrring in the casserrrole, and I'll be the one with the knife and forrrk."

Hen thought quickly — very quickly, as you do when you're about to be gobbled up.

"Dear Fox, I have a much better idea," she squawked. "Why don't you help me finish off my pot of nail soup? Seems a shame to waste a good soup when you're obviously so ravenous."

"Nail soup?" said Fox. "Never heard of it."

"It's delicious," said Hen. "Now, why don't you unpack those boxes while I bring the soup to the boil?"

With a loud haaarrrrrumph, he began to unpack the boxes. All six hundred and forty-two of them. Fox had just unpacked the last one when Hen brought him a spoonful of soup to taste.

"Bleurchhh!" he spat. "It's like hot, rusty water!"

"Mmm, you're quite right," murmured Hen. "Needs some salt to bring out the true nailishness of the soup. Tell you what, why don't you paint the living-room while I stir in the salt?"

Fox frowned. Something wasn't quite right here, but he didn't know what it was. Grumbling to himself he headed for the living-room.

He'd just put a final coat of gloss on the woodwork when Hen brought him another spoonful to try.

"Urrrchhhh!" he gagged. "Hot, rusty, salty water!"

"You could be right," mused Hen. "What we need are some root vegetables to give it some body… Could you be bothered to put up my kitchen units while I chop and peel the vegetables?"

Fox slitted his eyes and glared at Hen, but then his tummy growled and he decided to humour her. Armed with a bent screwdriver and a set of instructions in Serbo-Croat, he set to work.

He was just admiring his handiwork when Hen brought him another spoonful.

"Mmmmm, much better," he said.

"But…?" said Hen.

"Still a bit bland," said Fox.

"D'you know, I'm so glad you said that," said Hen. "I think so too. My instinct tells me that this soup needs a Mediterranean theme.

Be a love and sand the dining-room floor while I pick some beans and tomatoes for our soup."

Next time, vowed Fox, no matter what it tastes like, I'm eating it. He picked up a packet of miniscule nail files and headed for the dining-room.

Fox was lying panting in a corner of the freshly-sanded dining-room when Hen appeared with a spoonful of soup.

"Nearly there!" she said brightly, as the exhausted Fox took a sip.

"Great," he wheezed. "Perfect. Let's have it n…"

"Now, now," chided Hen. "Don't rush it. Rome wasn't built in a day, you know. I still have to add some herbs and a wee bit of parmesan. Look, why don't you light the fire and we can eat by firelight?"

"Where's the wood?" groaned Fox.

"Growing on that big tree outside," said Hen, passing him a tiny axe.

The fire was blazing merrily and the Fox was nearly asleep beside it when Hen appeared with another spoonful.

"Delicious," yawned Fox. "I don't suppose…?"

"NO," said Hen firmly. "It needs to simmer a while to soften the nail thoroughly. While we wait, you can sew some curtains for that window, so we can eat our soup by the fire without having to look at the darkness outside."

Dumbly, the Fox picked up a needle and began to sew full-length-box-pleated-fully-lined-with-pelmet curtains for Hen's window. Just as he'd finished and was pulling the curtains closed against the night, Hen arrived with a brimming pot of soup.

"Absolutely scrumptious!" said Fox, devouring his first bowl.

"Heaven in a pot!" he exclaimed after his third bowl.

"Who'd've thought a nail could taste this good?" he said, halfway through bowl eleven.

"Heavens, and so filling too," he gasped after bowl twenty-eight.

"I couldn't possibly manage another spoonful," he groaned as he emptied the pot.

"Oh well," said Hen with a wide grin. "Then it must be time for you to eat me." She sat back in her armchair by the fire, safe in the knowledge that the fox was far too full to eat anything more.

Aware that he'd been totally outfoxed, Fox looked at Hen, gave a huge belch, and with a furious roar, ran howling through the front door.

And was never seen again.

The Town Mouse and the Country Mouse

Houses for mouses,
or hices for mice,
range from tiny and cosy
to vast but not nice.

Thus it was with the Townmouse
(the most terrible snob)
who regarded her cousin
as a countrified slob.

"She's a hayseed, a turnip,
a moron, a twit,
but… I think I'll invite her
to town for a bit.

"A week in the city
would do her some good —
we'll do shopping and theatre
and eat some fine food.

"I'll fax her, I'll e-mail —
no, I'll phone her or write.
Or would carrier pigeon
appear more polite?

"I know, I'll deliver
this message myself;
for walking, they say,
is good for the helf."

And thus, two days later,
the Townmouse arrived;
grumpy and dusty
and frightfully tired.

The Countrymouse welcomed her,
drew her inside,
sat her down in an armchair
next to the fireside.

She smiled at her cousin
in her high heels and lace;
despite her long walk
not a hair out of place.

It's ever so flattering
to be invited
to visit the City —
why, I'd be delighted!

Outside, a lone pigeon
wheeled in the sky
while Countrymouse packed
and bid him goodbye.

"Take care of yourself,
and remember to write."
Waving wingtips and cooing,
the pigeon took flight.

The cousins set off
through cornfields and meadows;
one in her wellies,
the other, stillettoes.

The Townmouse was chatting
about make-up and diet;
her cousin smiled sweetly
but wisely kept quiet.

They came to the suburbs
as it started to rain;
in a torrent of water,
they swept down a drain.

The underground dwellers
were not much inclined
to extend hospitality
or be gentle and kind.

Battered and soggy
the mouse cousins emerged
at a vast intersection
where ten roads converged.

The Countrymouse felt
she was falling to bits.
The Countrymouse thought
that this place was the pits.

At last, at a building,
they spun through the door
and took the lift up
to the forty-fourth floor.

"Home sweet home," boasted Townmouse
with a wave of her wrist.
"Welcome back little Squeaky,"
an evil voice hissed.

"And a friend too! Delightful!
So yummy and choice!
A twin-pack, a double,"
continued the voice.

"I'll grill you and serve you
on a toasted brioche,
with white wine and salad —
now that would be posh."

Our two mice were frozen,
transfixed with fright;
they stared at the pussy
and then they took flight.

Stillettoes for running   Poor Townmouse was doomed,
are badly designed;   her shoes a disaster;
but wellies, though ugly,   Countrymouse fled away
   are better you'll find.   in her wellies far faster.

"Home sweet home — NOT!"
muttered Countrymouse grimly
as she climbed up the shaft
of a seldom-used chimney.

With the cat at her heels
she fled up to the stars,
coming out on the roof,
looking down on the cars.

"I'm done for, I'm finished,"
she thought, "I am doomed,"
unaware overhead
that a silhouette loomed.

A familiar pigeon
swooped down from the sky
    to help our poor mouse
    sprout wings and fly.

The pigeon flew in
and scooped Mouse in its claws,
    just avoiding the puss
    and its slavering jaws.

With a whoosh and a whuff
and a whirling of feathers,
Pigeon set the mouse down
on the softest of heathers.

"Oh, where am I now?"
asked the Mouse with a groan,
then opened her eyes
and found she was… HOME!

Cooing and billing
the briefest goodbye,
friend-pigeon flew off
into the night sky.

Travel they say's good
for improving the mind;
but staying put is safest
for the rurally inclined.

It is better to travel
in hope than arrive;
but better by far
is just to survive!

The Lion

and the Mouse

The lion sleeps,
the lion snores…
occasionally
the lion roars.

The mouse goes "Squeak!"
The mouse goes creep,
then Mouse wakes Lion
from growly sleep.

"I'll eat you up!"
the lion growls.
"Oh, don't do that!"
the rodent howls.

"I'm not a main course,
nor an hors d'oeuvre.
I think that you
should let me live."

"What a nerve
for one so small,"
the lion admires
the mouse's gall.

"I may be small,"
the mouse continues,
"but I'm sharp of tooth
and strong of sinews."

"My giddy aunt!
You do go on,"
and Lion gives
a great big yawn.

The mouse (alarmed
at those vast jaws)
struggles to escape
from Lion's paws.

But Lion shakes
and Lion shivers;
he trembles from
his mane to withers.

From close at hand
he hears loud noises;
clashing steel
and human voices.

Lion whispers
in Mouse's ear,
"Shoo! Run and hide!
Get outta here!"

Mouse blows Lion
a farewell kiss,
says, "I never will
     forget this."

Into the cave
with a wicked grin
a man with a sword
comes barging in.

Lion takes
a big deep breath;
prepares himself
for certain death.

More men pour in
with knives and net
saying, "O.K. Pussy,
in you get."

The men are cruel,
their deeds are murky,
and soon poor Lion's
trussed like a turkey.

Lion's tied,
Lion's cuffed;
Lion knows
he'll soon be stuffed.

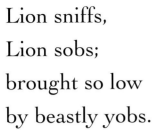

Lion sniffs,
Lion sobs;
brought so low
by beastly yobs.

The men are tired,
they've had their fun.
The men depart,
their day's work done.

Lion tries the knots
(they're all tied tight);
Lion heaves and tugs
with all his might.

He struggles, wriggles
(he's such a fighter);
but all he does
is tie them tighter.

Knots like sheepshanks,
grannys, reefs;
designed to test
a lion's teefs.

Lion chews till
his jaws ache.
At last he roars
"Give me a break!"

A tiny voice says
"Coo-eee! Guess who?"
It's that little mouse
to the rescue.

Mouse bites and nibbles,
chomps and chews,
and quickly turns
the lion loose.

The lion sobs,
the lion sniffs
and, grateful, gives
the mouse a kiss.

"I never thought
that one so small
could be of any
use at all."

Mouse says farewell,
shakes Lion's paw:
"Sometimes, my friend,
less is more."

The moral of this tale
for those who are wise
is: friends are friends
whatever their size.

"Ho hum," muttered Tortoise
in an unconcerned fashion,
"I'll just play it cool here —
there's no point in dashing."

One foot after the other
Tortoise plodded on,
pausing occasionally
to stifle a yawn.

Admiring the daisies,
enjoying the view,
taking time out for pit-stops
and going for a poo.

Three light years away
on a far distant star,
Hare shrieked to a standstill
thinking, "I've gone too far."

"But aren't I the greatest —
what panache, what aplomb.
What a drag though that I am
now so far from home."

Hare turned around
and retraced his path.
"I'll still win this race,"
he said with a laugh.

Meanwhile… here is Tortoise
just taking his time;
his beady eyes fixed
on the finishing line.

"Slow and steady will win,
not speedy and flash.
The plodder prevails over
the somewhat slapdash."

But what's that up ahead
with long floppy ears?
Tortoise's hunch is
it'll all end in tears.

Hare sets his alarm
for just forty winks.
"I'll snooze, then wake up
and still win," he thinks.

43

But Hare's sneaky plan
goes badly adrift;
when he wakes one day later
he's seriously miffed.

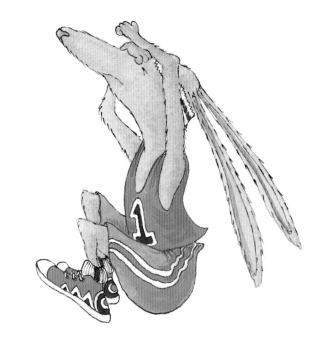

"Oh how could I be so
completely inept?
Tortoise won the race
while I overslept."

Hare had slept through the ringing,
the bells and the chimes.
Hare had forty winks,
but *thirty-six* times.

And here is our Tortoise –
The Winner! The Ace!
(For even no-hopers
sometimes win the race.)

The Tortoise being winner
against all the odds
proves that victory lies
in the lap of the gods.

Wolf and Rabbit

Old Grandpa Rabbit sat on the porch, rocking in the chair with his eight small grandchildren on his lap. One rabbit looks pretty much like another, and there were so many of them that Grandpa Rabbit never knew which grandchild was which. The little rabbits shook their heads till their ears flapped.

"Settle down," said Grandpa. "Stop wriggling, and then I'll begin."

Eight little cottontails squirmed, thirty-two arms and legs wriggled till all the little rabbits made themselves comfortable. Sixteen bright eyes gazed up at their Grandpa, waiting to hear his story.

"All this happened long before you were born. One far-away summer, Your Grandma met the Big Bad Wolf down by the lochside. Both of them were far too hot and tired to do anything other than wade into the loch and swim in companionable silence. When both were cool and refreshed, they climbed out of the water and dried themselves in the sun on the pebbly beach.

"I could run after you and eat you," remarked the Big Bad Wolf.

"But frankly, I can't be bothered."

"You'd have to catch me first," said Your Grandma. "And frankly, I bet you couldn't."

"Pah!" snorted the Big Bad Wolf. "I'm the fastest thing on four legs this side of the mountains."

"I don't think so," said Your Grandma. "I'm the speediest creature this side of the ocean."

"Whaaaat?" laughed the Big Bad Wolf. "Madam, you delude yourself. I'm the swiftest sprinter in the Northern Hemisphere."

"Mister Wolf," hissed Your Grandma. "I'm the best runner on earth. The only bit of you that is good at running is your tongue."

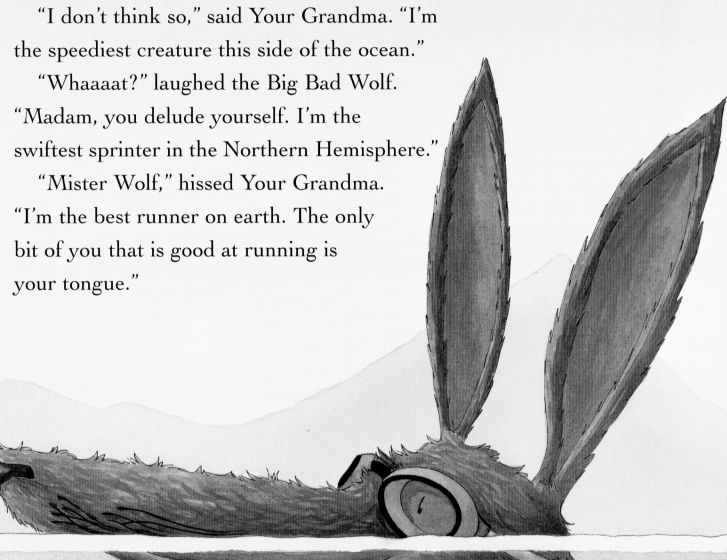

The Big Bad Wolf stood up, his yellow teeth bared in a snarl.

"This time m'girl, you've gone too far. Let us have a race right around the globe, and the winner gets to eat the loser."

Your Grandma just lay laughing in the sun, gazing up at the Big Bad Wolf.

"Oh my," she gasped. "I'll race you, me underground and you on top, but I'll have you on toast at the finish line."

"I'm just going home to chop some carrots for Rabbit stew," muttered the Big Bad Wolf. "Meet me here at first light and we'll see who's the fastest."

One of the grandchildren on Grandpa's lap burst into tears.

"Poor Grandma," he sobbed. "She's going to be eaten. With carrots!" Grandpa sighed. "How many times do I have to tell you? The story isn't over till we get to the end. Wait and see what happens and never assume the obvious. Now, where were we?"

"First light," prompted one small rabbit.

"Carrots," added another unhelpfully.

"At first light," continued Grandpa, "Your Grandma and the Big Bad Wolf met at the lochside."

"Why not save ourselves the effort and just let me eat you now?" suggested the Big Bad Wolf.

"Oh come now," said Your Grandma. "Where's your sense of adventure? Besides, if you eat me now, you'll never be sure if you were the fastest runner after all."

"PAH!" snorted the Big Bad Wolf. "I don't need to race to know that. However, have it your own way. Ready?"

Off they ran, Your Grandma down a burrow and the Big Bad Wolf straight across the meadow like a bolt of lightning. On he ran, mile after mile, heading in a northerly direction. The air grew cooler, the trees taller, but neither hide nor hair of Your Grandma did that Big Bad Wolf see until he was nearly at the North Pole. Popping out of a burrow in the snow up ahead were two furry little ears.

"Coo-eee, Mr Wolf!"

"Good grief!" panted the Big Bad Wolf. "However did you get here before me?"

"Easy when you know how," said the rabbit, disappearing back down the burr…

"Not 'the rabbit'," interrupted one of the grandchildren. "I think you mean, '… said Your Grandma, disappearing down the burrow'."

"No," said Grandpa firmly, "I don't. Never assume the obvious. It was your Great-Uncle Rebus, actually. But the Big Bad Wolf didn't know that. One rabbit looks pretty much like another. So, on they ran, the Big Bad Wolf loping past icebergs, over the North Pole, across the Siberian wastes and into Russia. Pausing in a small town to catch his breath, he caught sight of a depressingly familiar pair of ears.

"Greetings, Comrade Wolf," said the owner of the ears…

"Great-Uncle Rebus?" interrupted one of the grandchildren.

"NO," said Grandpa with just the faintest edge of irritation. "Your Cousin Vladimir, in fact. Don't interrupt."

"Phew!" said the Big Bad Wolf. "Surely that rabbit is going to tire out soon?"

On they raced, past the oil wells of Saudi Arabia (your Great-Great-Aunt Riyadh)

... down through Africa (your Cousin Owhatabele)

… across the Atlantic Ocean to Argentina (your Step-Cousin Santiago)

… across Antarctica (your Great-Aunt-Once-Removed Smorgasbrrr)

… and finally, via Iceland (your Second Cousin on Your Mother's side, Attityudsdottir) all the way back to Scotland.

Crawling through the meadow, the exhausted Big Bad Wolf dragged himself to the lochside. His paws were shredded, his coat mangy and his breath came in short pants.

"I'm pooped!" he gasped. "Where's that blooming bunny?" Up ahead, sunning herself on a rock with two pieces of toast ready by her side was…?"

"Our GRANDMA!" the grandchildren yelled.

"Indeed. Your Grandma," agreed Grandpa Rabbit. "And look! Here she comes now, with carrot cake and lemonade for us all."

54

Out from the kitchen came someone balancing a laden tray on her hip. "Grandma!" squeaked one of the small rabbits. "Did you eat the Big Bad Wolf on toast?"

"No," she said, placing the tray on a table near Grandpa's rocking chair. "Your Grandma is a vegetarian. Or, should I say, was?"

"Ggggrandmmma," quavered Grandpa, "whatever do you mean?"

"I'm not Your Grandma," roared the Bigger Badder Wolf, ripping off his lacy bonnet to expose a pair of long, furry, pointy ears. "I'm the Big Bad Wolf's youngest-nephew-thrice-removed, and you must never, never, ever assume the obvious."

There Was an Old Woman Who Swallowed a Fly

There was an old woman
who swallowed a fly.
She swallowed a fly!
(we don't know why)
Perhaps she'll die…

There was an old woman who swallowed a spider
that wriggled and tickled and squiggled insider.
She swallowed the spider to catch the fly,
She swallowed a fly! (we don't know why)
Perhaps she'll die…

56

There was an old woman who swallowed a frog,
a green-spotted frog complete with peat bog.
She swallowed the frog to catch the spider
that wriggled and tickled and squiggled insider.
She swallowed the spider to catch the fly.
She swallowed a fly! (we don't know why)
Perhaps she'll die…

There was an old woman who swallowed a trout
that slithered and slipped and tried to swim out.
She swallowed the trout to catch the frog,
a green-spotted frog complete with peat bog.
She swallowed the frog to catch the spider
that wriggled and tickled and squiggled insider.
She swallowed the spider to catch the fly.
She swallowed a fly! (we don't know why)
Perhaps she'll die...

There was an old woman who swallowed a swan
so pale and so quiet and so terribly wan.
She swallowed the swan to catch the trout
that slithered and slipped and tried to swim out.
She swallowed the trout to catch the frog,
a green-spotted frog complete with peat bog.
She swallowed the frog to catch the spider
that wriggled and tickled and squiggled insider.
She swallowed the spider to catch the fly.
She swallowed a fly! (we don't know why)
Perhaps she'll die…

There was an old woman who swallowed a fox
in a little red coat and little white socks.
She swallowed the fox to catch the swan
so pale and so quiet and so terribly wan.
She swallowed the swan to catch the trout
that slithered and slipped and tried to swim out.
She swallowed the trout to catch the frog,
a green-spotted frog complete with peat bog.
She swallowed the frog to catch the spider
that wriggled and tickled and squiggled insider.
She swallowed the spider to catch the fly.
She swallowed a fly! (we don't know why)
Perhaps she'll die…

There was an old woman who swallowed a bear.
Because of his claws, she had to take care.
She swallowed the bear to catch the fox
in a little red coat and little white socks.
She swallowed the fox to catch the swan
so pale and so quiet and so terribly wan.
She swallowed the swan to catch the trout
that slithered and slipped and tried to swim out.
She swallowed the trout to catch the frog,
a green-spotted frog complete with peat bog.
She swallowed the frog to catch the spider
that wriggled and tickled and squiggled insider.
She swallowed the spider to catch the fly.
She swallowed a fly! (now we'll never know why)
Perhaps she'll die…

There was an old woman who had just one question:
"Oh what can I take to cure indigestion?"
There was an old woman who swallowed a pill.
She swallowed the pill to stop feeling ill.
The pill was a horse-pill, she soon felt much worse.
Then she died, of course.

The Three Little Pigs

In a town nearby, lived three builders.
Despite them all being pigs, their work was very different.
Hamstraw only built houses from straw and grass.
His houses were very inexpensive, but they didn't last very long…

The second builder, Pigwood, only built houses from timber.

His houses were a little more pricey,
but they lasted for years…

The last builder, Porkstone, only built
houses in stone. Hardly anyone could afford
a Porkstone house, which is a pity because
they lasted for centuries.

One day Hamstraw was working at home when there was a
rustling at the door. Standing under the thatched porch was a wolf.

"EEEEK!" squeaked Hamstraw, and tied his door shut with
a rope made of cornstalks. Outside, the wolf tittered.

"Stalks and locks are not enough, I'll blow
your house down with one big PUFF."
And that was exactly what the wolf did.
He huffed and he puffed, and he BLEW
the house down.

Poor Hamstraw ran for his life, straight round to the house of his friend Pigwood, the builder. Pigwood was working on his kitchen table when Hamstraw arrived in a state of some alarm.

"The WOLF!" he gasped. "He's blown my house down! HELP! He's coming this way…"

And sure enough, there was a loud knock at the door. Pigwood peered out of an upstairs window. What he saw, standing on the deck, was not encouraging.

"EEEEK!" he squealed, slamming the window shut and running downstairs to hammer a plank of wood over his front door. Outside the wolf roared with laughter.

"Wood and nails will never last, I'll blow your house down with one big BLAST!"

And that was exactly what the wolf did.
He huffed and he puffed and he BLEW the house down.

Hamstraw and Pigwood ran for their lives, straight round to the house of their mutual friend, Porkstone, the builder. Porkstone was in his study doing his VAT return when Hamstraw and Pigwood fell through the door.

"The WOLF!" they sobbed. "He's blown our houses down. HELP! He's coming this way…"

And sure enough, there came a loud clang from the doorbell. Porkstone smiled. He knew his house couldn't be blown down, not with a PUFF, nor even a BLAST. However, there was the faint possibility that it could be blown UP. He peered through the spyglass.

And there was the wolf, lounging against one of Porkstone's statues by the front door, idly picking his teeth with a strand of fuse-wire. Seeing this, Porkstone dropped the portcullis, triple-locked the doors, shuttered the windows and headed for the kitchen, followed by his friends.

From outside, they could just hear the wolf cackling hysterically.

"Stone won't stop me, nor plaster dust. I'll blow this house flat with one big GUST."

And inhaling deeply, the wolf gave a huff and a puff and… nothing happened.

In the kitchen, Porkstone poured his friends a cup of tea, and stirred a pot of soup on the stovetop as if nothing untoward was happening. Overhead they heard the wolf clambering up a drainpipe onto the roof.

"Coo-eee," he called down the chimney. "Little piggy-wigs! I huffed and I puffed, but still your house stands, so now I'll PULL it apart with just my bare hands."

Then he hauled and he tugged… but still nothing happened.

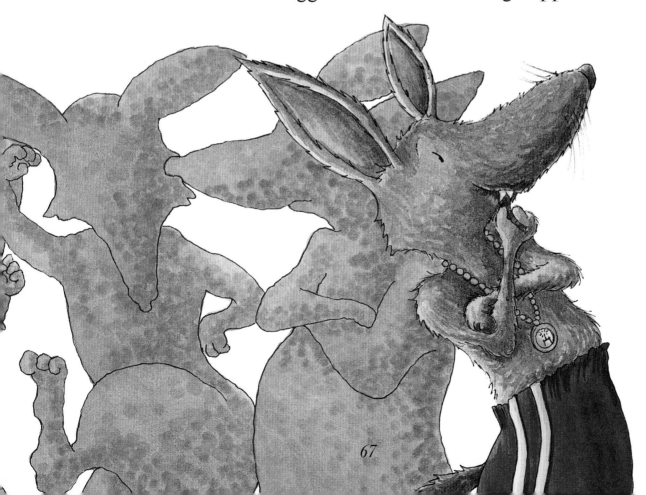

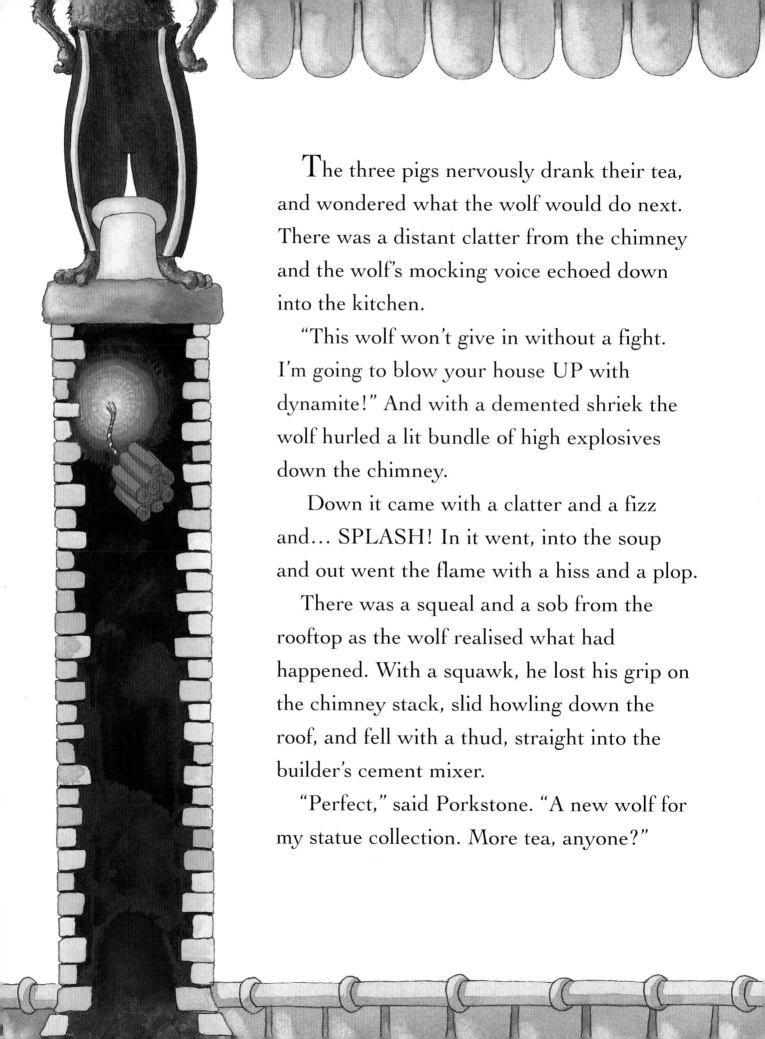

The three pigs nervously drank their tea, and wondered what the wolf would do next. There was a distant clatter from the chimney and the wolf's mocking voice echoed down into the kitchen.

"This wolf won't give in without a fight. I'm going to blow your house UP with dynamite!" And with a demented shriek the wolf hurled a lit bundle of high explosives down the chimney.

Down it came with a clatter and a fizz and... SPLASH! In it went, into the soup and out went the flame with a hiss and a plop.

There was a squeal and a sob from the rooftop as the wolf realised what had happened. With a squawk, he lost his grip on the chimney stack, slid howling down the roof, and fell with a thud, straight into the builder's cement mixer.

"Perfect," said Porkstone. "A new wolf for my statue collection. More tea, anyone?"

One Fat Cat

Purrfect was a perfect specimen of spoilt cat. She never lifted a paw to do anything, she ate her owner out of house and home, and she spent most of her time asleep on a velvet cushion in front of the fire.

On the rare occasions when Purrfect did wake up, it was usually only to complain.

"Bigger snacks NIAOWWWW," she'd moan.

"More salmon NIAOWWW!"

One day, left behind when her owner went to buy more cat food, Purrfect strolled into the kitchen to see if her bowl was indeed empty.

It was.

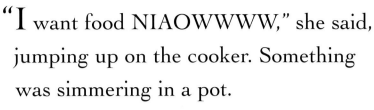

"I want food NIAOWWWW," she said, jumping up on the cooker. Something was simmering in a pot. Something smelled good.

"MMMMMMiaow," said Purrfect, lifting the lid on the pot. "No time like the present. I think I'll eat this soup and the pot too." She opened her mouth wide, wide, wide and tipped the pot and the soup into it. It was delicious. A bit chewy, but still absolutely scrumptious.

Just as Purrfect was polishing off the last of the pot lid, her owner returned home.

"Purrrfect!" she wailed. "You greedy beast. You've eaten the soup!"

"And the pot, too," admitted the cat. "And NIAOWWW I'm also going to eat YOU!"

And that spoilt, fat cat gobbled her owner up, licketty slurp, just like that!

"Oh my!" Purrfect patted her fat tummy, "I need a walk to aid my digestion." And out she went for some unaccustomed exercise. She strolled through the woods, and by and by she met Little Red Riding Hood, on her way back from her grandmother's house. The child stopped and stared at Purrfect.

"Good grief, pussy cat," she said. "Whatever have you eaten? You are so fat!"

"Well…," said Purrfect. "I ate my owner, her soup, and the pot too, and niaowww, I declare, I'm going to eat YOU!"

And that horrid, spoilt, fat cat gobbled Little Red Riding Hood up, gobblety slurp, just like that!

"Hey!" came a shout. "You can't do that! Spit her back out, you horrid, fat cat!"

Running towards Purrfect were the three little pigs, waving and shouting.

"Hmmm," said Purrfect. "I ate the girl in the hood (mmm, she tasted quite good), I ate my owner, her soup, and the pot too, and niaowww, little pigs, I'm going to eat YOU!"

Down Purrfect's throat went the three little pigs, squealing and squeaking, hoggitty slurp, just like that!

"I need a drink niaoww," moaned Purrfect, dragging her bloated tummy over to the riverbank. She stretched out on a rock, lowered her head to the river and stopped. There, reflected in the water, was a huge lion leaning over Purrfect's shoulder, jaws a-slaver.

"Whatever have you been eating?" it roared. "What a rrrevoltingly rrrotund cat you are."

"Rrreally?" said Purrfect. "I'm rrrotund because I ate three little swine (they slid down just fine), I ate a girl in a hood (she tasted quite good), I ate my owner, her soup, and I ate the pot too, and niaoww, Dear Sir, I'm going to eat YOU!"

Can you believe it? Down that lion went, growlitty slurp, just like that!

"Poor lion," said a voice. "Still… I'm safe. You can't eat me – I come in a shell." Lolling in the shallows was a tortoise wearing an unbelievably smug grin on its face.

"Says who?" said Purrfect, pouncing on the tortoise and mumbling in between mouthfuls. "I ate the lion, along with its Roar (I can't help thinking I've had lion before…), I ate three little swine (they slid down just fine), I ate the girl in the hood (she tasted quite good), I ate my owner, her soup, and the pot too, and as you might have observed, I am niaowww eating YOU!"

And indeed, crunchitty slurp, there went tortoise, just like that!

Distended beyond recognition, Purrfect rolled along the riverbank till she came to the edge of a freshly ploughed cornfield. There, eating her lunch, was the Little Red Hen.

"Greetings corpulent cat," she said. "My! You are the fattest feline I've ever seen…"

"ENOUGH for niaowww," groaned Purrfect. "From the top: I ate the tortoise and its shell (perhaps that's why I feel so unwell), I ate the lion, along with its Roar (I can't help thinking I've had lion before…), I ate three little swine (they slid down just fine), I ate the girl in the hood (she tasted quite good), I ate my owner, her soup, and the pot too, and, regretfully, I am also going to eat YOU!"

With a flutter of feathers, down went the Little Red Hen, squawkitty slurp, just like that!

"Urghh," moaned Purrfect. "I feel awful. I must lie down." She collapsed in a vast heap and lay burping and belching in the midday sun.

By and by there came a weeping procession of animals, all following a cart, upon which lay a coffin. To Purrfect's astonishment, the cart hit a bump in the road, the coffin bounced about, and out from under its lid flew an enormous fat fly.

Seizing upon the flatulent cat as an ideal
site for buzzing, the fly began to orbit poor Purrfect.

"Bzzzzzzzzz," said the fly.

"Go away," muttered the cat.

"Nozzzzzzzz," said the fly, buzzing and zizzing around
Purrfect's ears.

"Get LOST!" yelled the cat.

"Zzzzshan't," said the fly.

The fat cat stood up. The fat cat hauled her stomach out of a nearby
ditch and propped herself against a tree. The fat cat burped three times.

"RRRRIGHT," said the fat cat, "read my lips. I ate the Little Red
Hen (shan't do that again), I ate the tortoise and its shell (perhaps

that's why I feel so unwell), I ate the lion, along
with its Roar (I can't help thinking I've had lion before...),
I ate three little swine (they slid down just fine), I ate the girl
in the hood (she tasted quite good), and... I ate my owner, her
soup, and pot too, and niaowww (burrrrp) I am going to have
to eat YOU!"

How wrong could a pussycat be?

The fly had no intention of being anyone's lunch.
It buzzed and it bizzed, it flipped and it flapped and finally it zigged
and it zagged right up to the top of a tree, pursued by Purrfect.
Trying not to look down, the fat cat took one last swipe at
the fly and...

AAAAARGH

and

EEEEEEEEK

and

Slappetty splat, poor Purrfect fell to the ground and burst wide open. Out rolled the Little Red Hen, the tortoise in its shell, the lion with its Roar, the three little pigs, Little Red Riding Hood, and Purrfect's owner, clutching her soup pot.

And do you know what?

The soup was still hot!